MW01178662

Allo

Running the Race: Jesus and Success

Written and compiled
by Sarah M. Hupp

Designed by Arlene Greco

Inspire Books is an imprint of Peter Pauper Press, Inc.

Photographs have been licensed by The Image Bank®.
End-sheet photo copyright © 1983 Andre Gallant
Interior photos:
Page 4 copyright © 1991 Hans Wendler
Page 13 copyright © 1991 John Kelly
Page 20 copyright © 1994 Philip De Renzis
Page 29 copyright © 1995 Grant V. Faint
Page 37 copyright © 1996 Eric Shweikardt
Page 46 copyright © 1993 Grant V. Faint
Page 55 copyright © 1992 Patti McConville
Page 64 copyright © 1990 Kaz Mori
Page 71 copyright © 1990 Nick Nicholson
Page 77 copyright © 1993 Ross M. Horowitz

For permissions please see page 80.

Running
the
Race:

Jesus
and Success

What does the Lord require of you? To act justly and to love mercy and to walk humbly with your God.

Micah 6:8 NIV

the newest buzzword
is success.

No need for what is
second best.

Only the topmost slot will do;

Ol' #1 is better than you.

But there is something
very wrong

With that worn-out,
old selfish song.

Success that only puts
"me first"

Will only bring a life of hurt.

So God shows us
a better way—

Sent his son Jesus
here to say,

"Run the race and follow me;

Then you'll live successfully."

SARAH MICHAELS

Jesus said: "Everyone who has left houses or brothers or sisters or father or mother or wife or children or lands, for My name's sake . . . "

MATTHEW 19:29 NKJV

" . . . shall receive a
hundredfold, and inherit
eternal life."

MATTHEW 19:29 NKJV

Jesus said
"Whoever does not
carry his own cross and
come after Me cannot
be My disciple."

LUKE 14:27 NASB

An upright man
can never be a
downright failure.

E. C. McKenzie

Of all failings,
the ugliest is the lust
for personal success.

DAGOBERT D. RUNES

money measures only prosperity. Success is a matter of character.

THE LITTLE GAZETTE

At the Judgment Day we will
all stand before the
Almighty. Then we will truly
know which ones he
considers successful, and
which ones will feel his ire.

Denying ungodliness
and worldly lusts, we should
live soberly, righteously,
and godly in the
present age.

TITUS 2:12 NKJV

For bodily exercise profiteth little: but godliness is profitable unto all things, having promise of the life that now is, and of that which is to come.

I Timothy 4:8 kjv

Put your trust in the Lord your God, and you will be established. Put your trust in His prophets and succeed.

2 Chronicles 20:20 NASB

Even if you
should suffer for
what is right, you
are blessed.

1 PETER 3:14 NIV

Success is to be measured not by wealth, power, or fame, but by the ratio between what a man is and what he might be.

H. G. WELLS

Many times we must

keep working, striving,

walking and believing

when the way seems dark

and the path unclear . . .

. . . Yet when we persevere and trust God's direction, believing that He will work all things out for our good; this in itself is true success.

Jesus said:

"Whoever finds his life

will lose it,

and whoever loses his life

for my sake will find it."

MATTHEW 10:39 NIV

Jesus said:

"What does it profit

a man to gain the whole

world, and forfeit

his soul?"

Jesus said: "Whoever serves me must follow me."

JOHN 12:26 NIV

Jesus said: "Many that
are first shall be last;
and the last first."

MARK 10:31 KJV

You can't carve your way
to success with
cutting remarks.

E. C. McKenzie

People often credit
themselves for their
successes, and God
for their failures.

E. C. McKenzie

The adage, "Bloom where you're planted" applies to success. If you want to make good somewhere, why not start where you are?

he sought his God and
worked wholeheartedly.
And so he prospered.

2 CHRONICLES 31:21 NIV

Those who cling to
worthless idols forfeit
the grace that could
be theirs.

JONAH 2:8 NIV

The race is not to the swift,

Nor the battle to the strong,

Nor bread to the wise,

Nor riches to men

of understanding . . .

Ecclesiastes 9:11 NKJV

nor favor to men of skill;
But time and chance
happen to them all.

Ecclesiastes 9:11 nkjv

May he give you the desire
of your heart and make all
your plans succeed.

PSALMS 20:4 NIV

Our successes most often lie on the other side of our failures.

O Lord of hosts,
how blessed is the man
who trusts in Thee!

Psalms 84:12 NASB

Oo not pray for tasks equal
to your powers. Pray for
powers equal to your tasks.
Then the doing of your work
will be no miracle; but you
shall be a miracle.

PHILLIPS BROOKS

Blessed is the man that walketh not in the counsel of the ungodly, nor standeth in the way of sinners, nor sitteth in the seat of the scornful. But his delight is in the law of the LORD . . . and whatsoever he doeth shall prosper.

PSALMS 1:1-3 KJV

You will prosper,
if you take care
to fulfill the statutes
and judgments with
which the LORD
charged Moses.

1 CHRONICLES 22:13 NKJV

the LORD God is a sun and shield; the LORD gives grace and glory; no good thing does He withhold from those who walk uprightly.

PSALMS 84:11 NASB

Delight thyself
also in the LORD; and he
shall give thee the desires
of thine heart.

PSALMS 37:4 KJV

Although our task
be humble,

Let us work each day
with care;

For we may not know
God's purpose,

Or why He placed us there.

HENRY B. KNOX

Those who rise to the
headiest heights in any field
aren't necessarily the ones
with the greatest natural
talent. They're the diligent
few who put in the hours.
They work hard. And then
they work harder.

JOHN E. ANDERSON

try not to
become a man of
success but rather
try to become a
man of value.

ALBERT EINSTEIN

God in wisdom
knows a way,

And that is sure,
let come what may,

Who does God's work
will get God's pay.

UNKNOWN

Do not let this Book
of the Law depart from your
mouth; meditate on it
day and night, so that
you may be careful to
do everything written in it.
Then you will be
prosperous and successful.

Joshua 1:8 NIV

make yourself
indispensable and you
will move up. Act as though
you are indispensable
and you will move out.

UNKNOWN

I have been young,
and now am old;
yet have I not seen the
righteous forsaken, nor his
seed begging bread.

PSALMS 37:25 KJV

They who seek
the LORD shall not
be in want of any
good thing.

PSALMS 34:10 NASB

ʄailure is only
the opportunity to begin
again more intelligently.

HENRY FORD

Ready, set, go!
Life's race has now begun.
The way is clear;
The path is set;
It's time for us to run.

Moving on up
The ladder of success;
Just don't forget

God's law of love—
Keep Faith! For that's the test.

The end's in sight!
We're running faithfully.
We'll have success
And happiness
If we but follow Thee.

SARAH MICHAELS

Ɗesire that ye might be filled with the knowledge of his will in all wisdom and spiritual understanding; That ye might walk worthy of the Lord . . .

COLOSSIANS 1:9-10 KJV

. . . being fruitful
in every good work,
and increasing in the
knowledge of God.

Colossians 1:10 kjv

happy is he
who has the God of Jacob
for his help, whose hope
is in the LORD his God.

PSALMS 146:5 NKJV

Do not merely look out
for your own personal
interests, but also for the
interests of others.

PHILIPPIANS 2:4 NASB

Don't be discouraged
if you are not finding the
acceptance and success you
desire today. Your success
story is still being written!

the choices you make
today will define what
you will become tomorrow.
Choose wisely;
choose well.

the road to success

follows three paths:

aspiration, inspiration,

and perspiration.

If you want to climb

the ladder of success,

you must begin

at the bottom.

Be ye steadfast,
unmoveable, always
abounding in the work of
the Lord, forasmuch as
ye know that your labour is
not in vain in the Lord.

I Corinthians 15:58 KJV

All hard work
brings a profit, but mere talk
leads only to poverty.

PROVERBS 14:23 NIV

Sow to yourselves in righteousness, reap in mercy; break up your fallow ground: for it is time to seek the LORD, till he come.

HOSEA 10:12 KJV

The noble man devises noble plans; and by noble plans he stands.

Isaiah 32:8 NASB

no man is
justified in doing evil
on the ground
of expediency.

THEODORE ROOSEVELT

Do you find the door
to success locked before you?
Only God holds the key.
Gain God's perspective and
he will unlock the door.

Do not allow success
to turn your head;
you will only find yourself
looking in the
wrong direction.

Be strong and very
courageous. Be careful
to obey all the law my
servant Moses gave you;
do not turn from it to the
right or to the left, that
you may be successful
wherever you go.

JOSHUA 1:7 NIV

Do you not know that those who run in a race all run, but only one receives the prize? Run in such a way that you may win.

1 Corinthians 9:24 NASB

a man's gift makes room
for him, and brings him
before great men.

PROVERBS 18:16 NKJV

Whatever your
hand finds to do,
do it with your might.

ECCLESIASTES 9:10 NKJV